Further I

These poems speak, with incandescent candor and uncanny insight, for everyone whom life has ever ambushed, who discovers she was not who she thought she was or was supposed to be, for every woman changed by giving birth. Alicia Jo Rabins' *Fruit Geode* opens to a brilliant ripeness—a daring 21st century vision informed by an ancient wisdom.

—Eleanor Wilner

Pregnancy is literal embodiment, and Alicia Jo Rabins' *Fruit Geode* is a translation of this experience into literary embodiment. She scouts out for us the perfect metaphors: "slot machine," "seed-lined ark," "black pond." I love the new-mother hyper-attention here, to the mournful and the sublime, the sacred and profane, the ancient and brand-new. "Now that I have been / broken, / I can begin," Rabins writes, and I recommend this book to anyone beginning to learn how to parent, how to be gentle, how to awaken to mortality.

—Arielle Greenberg

Also by Alicia Jo Rabins

Divinity School

FRUIT GEODE

Alicia Jo Rabins

Augury Books * New York

Fruit Geode
© 2018 by Alicia Jo Rabins

ISBN: 978-0-9995012-0-7

Cover and interior design by Shanna Compton.
Edited by Kate Angus.

Cover art: Pomegranate (Punica granatum) from *Pomona Italiana* (1817–1839) by Giorgio Gallesio (1772–1839) / Gemstones by Walter Wild, from: Wild, Georg O. *Praktikum der Edelsteinkunde.* Franckh'sche Buchhandlung, Stuttgart, 1936. Used with permission of Franckh-Kosmos Verlags.

Published in the United States of America by:
Augury Books
154 N 9th St #1
Brooklyn, NY 11249
AuguryBooks.com; info@augurybooks.com

Distributed to the trade by Small Press Distribution (SPD)
www.spdbooks.org

Library of Congress Cataloging-in-Publication Data
Names: Rabins, Alicia Jo, author.
Title: Fruit geode / by Alicia Jo Rabins.
Description: First edition. | Brooklyn, NY : Augury Books, [2018]
Identifiers: LCCN 2018019412 | ISBN 9780999501207 (pbk. : alk. paper)
Subjects: LCSH: Motherhood--Poetry.
Classification: LCC PS3618.A3245 A6 2018 | DDC 811/.6--dc23
LC record available at https://lccn.loc.gov/2018019412

First Edition

for Aaron, without whom none of this

CONTENTS

BEAUTIFUL VIRUS

Like arsenic in chocolate

Like a pea shoot in mud

You broke me open

Into death-in-life

A beautiful virus

Uncontrollably growing

As the morning glories

Climb the raspberries

That choke the grapes that

Overrun the spinach

What I mean to say is

Knocked off the pedestal

Of wholeness

Now I watch you breathe

In your miniature

Flamingo pajamas

TO GROW WISE

One day I awoke

to find myself

in an unfamiliar body:

knees like tree trunks,

passages in my belly,

eyes two pools of tea.

I began to understand

the two sides of

this sheath I wear:

an old used suit,

and the chariot

I ride through blessed

days and nights.

I began to feel the ones

who will live

millennia from now

hiding inside my pockets

like poppy seeds.

By this time

I could barely remember

the body I wore before.

I thought to myself,

now that I have been

broken,

I can begin.

BOY, GIRL, ANGEL, GOLEM

I am a slot machine
I am a globe
spin me
put your finger down
buy a guidebook buy a ticket
find a cheap hotel
in the Old City
meet me on the roof
for a drink
show me the lights from above
read my tongue my bellyshape
boy, girl, angel, golem
you dissolve my allegiance
I forget who I was
I learn to say my new name
the globe collapses
to a dot
the dot is you
I'll follow you anywhere

MAGIC MOVES SIDE TO SIDE

Gravity moves up and down,

magic side to side.

I stood beneath the traffic light

waiting for you.

It was sheep-shearing season

and I your sheep.

I knew this meeting was the fulcrum:

young me to old me,

old me to new me.

As a mother carries her young

daughter to the toilet

in the middle of the night

to help her body learn

to hold its liquids,

I carry myself,

I teach myself when to hold,

when to spill.

GEODE

The plagues we wished upon ourselves

With aloe juice and cayenne

The planets we strained to reach

That was how being young tasted

Each of us a geode looking to be cracked

And to crack each other open

Over and over

I am no longer young except to those who are older

In the way that youth moves along

The conveyor belt

At a consistent distance

I drink water now

I try to be gentle

The years crack you open enough

PASSENGER

seed-lined ark

mother papaya

whale belly

my little Jonah

dear passenger

as a plane

I carry you

to be a woman

is to be a wall

with a hole

to be a human

a hole with walls

even the rain

tastes red to you

the strawberries

are over but the sun

keeps shedding

my blood doubles

to keep you

aloft

LAMENT FOR THE PRE-PREGNANCY CITY

vessel yes miraculous yes but sometimes

I miss the office above the city

where we fucked diligently

it was our homework and we

were good little boys and girls

wine and cheese on Tuesday nights

instant miso in the break room

it was our spaceship

well as much ours as our bodies

which is to say not for long

what do you think

will I remember this body

the next time around

as I remember that office

its scars its hidden corners

and the way the lights

undressed themselves each night

before my hungry eyes

rectangular yellow butterfly wings

in the oil slick of summer

wearing the body I used to love

in the city I used to love

MATERIA MEDICA

when Achilles was born
his mother held him by the heel
and dipped him in a vat of yarrow tea
to protect him from harm
many years later he died
of a wound on the ankle where
her fingers touched him
and the yarrow could not

squirrel's tail   warrior plant
thousand leaf   hero

I too print mortality on my daughter
show her the white yarrow
growing beside the concrete
when she was born a masked doctor
held her by the heel
I heard her yowl before I saw her
the wound of birth tore us in two
we regarded each other

across unfamiliar air
we regard each other still

daughter we are
sometimes girls sometimes
crones or sisters
or friends
I teach you what I know
I make a tea-bath for you

of yarrow's
thousand leaves

witch   warrior
doctor   mother

THE VAGINA HEALER

The vagina healer had a vision

With her gloved hand inside me

She saw my water break

Not in a magnetic field of hospital white

But under the apple tree

Between the garden boxes

"Energetic birth" she called it

She said I could rewrite the script

So here it is:

I am a fruit geode

My midwife's name is Mary

I give birth in a garden

To a grandfather

Vernix

Light

Apples

REMEMBER HOW WE PLANNED TO GET MARRIED AND HAVE CHILDREN?

Remember that winter
When you were still alive?
The cold of outer space
When the door opened
And the warmth of our bodies
When it closed?
Remember the branches
Out the window
Black with ice
And how you loved
To read their runes
Against the sky?
How you hated
When I smoked cigarettes
And I hated
When you smoked pot
But we understood each other:
I needed to breathe
And you needed a way
To tame the blue lines
That shot out from your head
Like an invisible
Crown of feathers
Only we could see.
Remember how we planned
To get married and have children?
And then we didn't get married
Didn't have children
Six years later you left for good

And no one can tell me how.
It had something to do
With your suffering
Which we both knew was part
Of your job description as a prophet.
Still *I'm sorry for your loss,*
Sorry for all of it.
I know you can't stay long
So let me tell you the secret:
Sometimes I look at my son
And see your face.

THE DIAGONAL CARRIES US

Sometimes you are the man kneeling in the field

And sometimes you are the angel rising in the field

Sometimes you are the baby sleeping with crossed ankles

And sometimes you are the mother crying for no discernible reason

Except that one day the baby will die

The angel rising behind him on a diagonal

The diagonal carrying us all along even now

On this stage, this bed, this field where I kneel

Blind to the future rising behind me

MY NEW FACE

I too was pretty once

I too pulled my hair up

When I walked

My steps had a sharp sound

Like a drum kit

In the hands of a jazz-trained

Rock drummer

When my face broke into pieces

I picked them up and carried them

In my skirts

Across the field to you

To show you

My new face

Ana lights four candles

Above my head

Do you like it,

Moon?

Can I join

The circle now?

OPEN WHITE SEA

once life was a blank

white sea with blue lines

every day I set my sails

until I gave the blank page

to the embryo of a person

the open white sea filled in

with colors and chores

sacred rectangle a secret now

a name whispered once a year

on the holiest day

rarer than sex

I am not complaining

I become the page

that holds the story

with responsibility a relief

of lines written

in mint and chamomile

time, a game of whack-a-mole

people pay for the pleasure

of playing

at the fair or in the garden

with yellow calendula

and tiny cups of tea

ANCESTOR ALPHABET

I see the shape of the Alef and the shape of the Lamed

I see the shape of the final Tzadi and the shape of the Hay

I see the shape of your Nose and the shape of your Hands

Which are the same shape as your father's Hands

We first kissed in a Bar after he gave me a small plastic Fish

Purchased in Chinatown now he is cleaning up the Kitchen

Listening to a Podcast I see the shape of the dead Tulips

Beginning to crumple upon themselves in the Vase

I hear a fake English Accent it's a Comedy Podcast

I hear Anxiety beneath the listening I see petals turn Brown

I see Worms under the Earth I see many Leaves I see Toys and Books

A rumpled Couch a Bowl of Pink Salt with a Tiny Spoon

O Asherah keep us safe

I see Heaven I see Bed I see Mirror I see Porridge

I feel the Ancients watching us I watch you as you sleep

TO MY MIDWIFE

you sat in the
rocking chair
and watched
to keep me safe

you checked your phone
you checked my cervix
when it had gone on
for too long

you drove me
to the hospital
on all fours
in the trunk

of your hatchback
as I screamed
over the speed bumps
so much for homebirth

strangers watched
in the ER as you
braced your body
against the wall

so I could lean on you
oh Mary
now I'm alone with my baby
and you are elsewhere

your hand inside
some other mother

PIG IN A BLANKET

my little blueberry

my pig in a blanket

for you I've become

dangling grapes

for you I put on this

fat suit

and filled my body

with blood

sweet lochia

red on white

for weeks afterward

for you scans

and scalpel

for you boxes of diapers

arrive daily

you honor me

with the name

mother

although in my heart

I am both vain

& ugly

SITUATION REPORT

The yard has become an ice-planet.
The rosemary coated in crystal armor.

Everything different and the same.
I once wrote, "An ice planet

Can only be entered alone,"
Or something like that.

And I think of this as I navigate
The moon-yard in my boots,

Sliding a little, cracking, breaking through.
I still think it true,

Ice is solitude made material,
I am not the person I was,

Even my words wear the crystal
Armor so that I am not embarrassed

To quote myself,
This ice planet being a place

Where I regard my former life
With a distant affection,

As an astronaut
Looks through a porthole

At the small green planet
Where she used to live.

I SUCK YOUR FEVER OUT

Through forehead kisses and spit it back to Jupiter

The angry-red has taken hold in our house we do not sleep more
than an hour

I know the temperature inside your rectum I know how to
smooth your baby head of hair I know one day you will leave
me as you must

I dream of more babies more pregnancies Oh to drown

To annihilate myself to be vessel to create to make something of
myself at last

But this is almost more than we can handle already says my
husband he's right we won't

Though their baby selves haunt me nightly calling *mama mama
bring me down to earth*

Damp washcloth on your head fever kisses on your fat cheeks I
suck your fever out I keep you here with us

I could throw myself from a window to keep you from getting
any more beautiful

MOTHERSICKNESS

O morning

O blue eyes

O David Bowie

O fighter pilot training overhead

O sketch comedian sister in law

O stretched out underwear

O baby formula

O rhythm

O Mom and Dad

O twisted humor

O feng shui

O election

O despair

O alternate social network

O dream of escape

Escape

Escape

WHEN I LIVED IN NEW YORK

This matzah ball soup
Reminds me of my grandmother
I'm so close to her here in Brooklyn city of her birth

Darling as she called everyone
Let's be sentimentalists together
And forget about her personality disorder

Forget her in the attic on St Marks Avenue
Thinking her baby was a bouquet of flowers
Instead regard the mama bird

Feeding her openmouthed chicks
Who is the worm I am the worm
Who is the mother I am the mother

Juggling too many lifetimes to count
So I let them drop like planets
Marbles falling on the carpet of ocean

If I were a nightingale
I'd always say the right thing
Instead I am hedgehog sweetgum ball prickly pear

And I stick my edges into the bullshit
Politeness of the West Coast
When I lived in New York I kept my exterior polished

I thought the pigeons were nightingales
Reflection friend past self in the subway glass
O the mornings I wasted

Reading about how to give birth

BABIES IN THE APOCALYPSE

I'd rather not know the solstice

Is going to fall apart

Like the rest of what we hold sacred

In the amphitheater we watched

Heron, story, glaze

We knew this might happen

But still we called you forth

With mandrakes

And red clover

IN BETWEEN LIFETIMES

so I exited the jungle of pink

time beating in my veins

carried an upright bass down the stairs

music in your fingers

it was a precarious existence

mosaic around the edges

between female and male

where we traded back and forth

the currency of shame & razors

cello, wings, salt in the cuts,

and genderless astronauts

I might have been Greek

or Egyptian or Sumerian

or Hebrew looking for you

MERCATOR PROJECTION

inside me, two golden ovaries

my singing bowls

beside me, husband

two golden bells

and a mallet to tap

the bowls awake

outside me, the flat surface

swells to a globe

a destiny map

too large to hold

memory

a six-sided cell

always under construction

space added on

room by tiny room

to build a hive

ISIS LACTANS

typing one handed

while you

comfort   nurse

while I

one handed   type

while you

comfort   nurse

THE MONASTERY OF MOTHERHOOD

it's hard to face
my ugly old self again
whether by the pig farm
or metropolitan crossroads
but the hardest is alone
with children
I'd cut my lungs out for her
but then I spray her
in the face with the hose
when she claws for the baby
and so in the monastery
of motherhood I find the devil
in my own heart
and God too in the form
of El Shaddai
the breast-God
nursing as I write
and oh how the helpless babe
grows into an angry being
I pray they'll be better than me
I've done my best so far and
been ashamed of it

WILL & TESTAMENT

To you, preverbal

Larva, dear homunculus,

I give the future

Willingly

I give it all to you

As you one day will

Give it to your lover

Will you think

Of me then

I hope not

That's not your job

MORNINGS DISSOLVE

And before I capture them

Eggs crack and buds break through

Virgin branches

Endings inside petal and yolk

Kindergarten in the cradle and casket

In the marriage bed

No one understands more than you

Kindness

Each evening I am sorry for planting

Twenty dormant seeds

Of mistake

And yet

You wake up calling for me

WE LEARN TO BE HUMAN

I attended the online seminar on shame

it helped for a minute

more importantly I've been loving

the goddess for a long time like

five thousand years now and these

hiccups in my groin are a sign

she'll be here when it's time

now in a white t-shirt you go

to bed husband you started as a seed

I'll meet you when I'm done

taking off my makeup we

learn to go to bed to put on

eyeliner we learn to be human

when we don't get what we want

you too started as a seed and now

my son I feel your fingers

uncurling against my center

from the inside

like a fern

HOME BIRTH VIDEOS

as it turns out closely

resemble amateur porn

in the church of my heart too

the choir squirts

sometimes red sometimes white

sometimes the body is blue

she cries out

help me   no no it's OK

somebody help me   no no I'm OK

the red tapestry

hangs dumbly on the wall

its seven hundred tiny mirrors

watch the little head

emerge bluely

from the crying woman

I too am a crying woman

seven hundred thousand

views & this is how I finally learn

what the body is

a sheath

that cries out

again and again

GRIEF COMES IN WAVES LIKE
EVERYTHING ELSE

and the thing about a wave is that it dissolves
tuna fish sandwiches and potato chips

birth-pains of the Messiah
the body's twelve mouths open

to let go the muted greens
and grays of familiar grief

until the ancestors
smile from their graves as

we hold hands across the birthing-tub
dissolving then calm then another gathering

all the way and I glow incandescent
then the dimmer down again

broken geode on the windowsill
my mother's sweet iced tea through a straw

MOTHER'S DAY

When the sandbox is overturned

And the cucumber shoots are heavy with particulate

I chant summer summer summer

And walk upstairs

This is how it is now:

I lose my patience over and over

Only to find it waiting for me

Calling me

Not by my name

But by the name *mother*

MY WHOLE VAGINA LIFE

like living in a hollowed-out tree

visited by woodland creatures and bloodred crystals

there were small babies up there waiting

mornings and midnights

it led me to conference rooms and cedar groves

sometimes it hurt a lot, or itched

honestly it probably had a lot to do with your choosing me

in the end nobody came out of it

they took the escape hatch

sometimes it was a kelp sculpture

once I wrote a poem about it that nobody liked

I was always intrigued by the sweet slippery smells

corners where I used to hide and smoke

or read behind the unadorned bushes

near the high school

adolescence is a pomegranate

translated through

the language of that cave

marriage is a mango and

death a durian

in that fruity tunnel around which

I revolve night and day

CRADLE CAP

I won't be able to sweep the bits of skin from your neck
I'll be dead and gone I won't be able to help you then
The umbilical stump withers and falls off
Tiny man in my arms

I can't stop thinking
About you as an old man

Your scalp will be dry just like now

EXIT INTERVIEW

She said, you are underqualified for this.

You will have others but not this one.

She said, you are overqualified for this.

You don't even know how to change a diaper.

How to wrap it up tight so the poop stays inside.

She said, you still flinch when shit gets on your hands.

Come back when you're done with that.

Come back when you're done being precious.

Come back when you're not pretty anymore,

When you grow into your own pain.

Then we can talk.

I DREAM OF MY BABY SLEEPING
WHILE HE SLEEPS

Of my college girlfriend, tall redheaded and now pregnant in
   London

Of blood on my underwear and copper IUDs falling from the sky

Of my baby sleeping while he sleeps

Of the ghost of the woman who dressed her children for Sunday
   School and left them on the stoop

Cambridge dreams and Revere dreams and Brooklyn dreams

I dream of shooting the yappy dog

Of fuchsia pink and butter yellow

Settling over the sky like Tuesday

MESSAGE FROM EARTH

A mother knows how to praise time

The medium that paints us

Each day slightly differently

Here on this planet

Taste of elk

Smell of sheep

Finger-feel of leaves & roots

Petals and sepals earned one by one

Licorice for the throat

Comfrey for the joints

The body doubles in on itself

Mullein for the lungs

Like a restaged epic

Calendula and yarrow for the skin

Motherwort for the heart

This month you want to be

An astronaut my daughter

When you go into space

Take these with you

Tell them this planet was beautiful

POND, COSMOS

I am a starry cosmos

lying on the floor

I am a black pond

lying on the floor

I am a starry cosmos

MEMOIR

Once I commanded you, dear reader, to kiss my snood. I was young and brave.

And once I stood openhearted at the top of a mountain. I was afraid of heights. Around my ankles, millennia swirled.

Once I was very old and could not speak, only watch the people moving around me—so busy, so fast.

Once I helped keep a flame lit, I held it aloft, I passed it to the next runner.

I could not breathe. We had to turn back across the bridge.

Once I sat next to my love in the movie theater with disposable 3D glasses on our separate noses and watched time made material while eating popcorn and drinking chemicals.

Once I loved the mall more than any place on earth.

Once I loved cigarettes.

Once I loved my best friend.

Once my best friend loved me.

Once I used to sit and tap, tap, tap, waiting for the gates to unlock, for the fires to subside.

And once, no, twice I lay on the birthing-table and a stranger
  cut me open, my body falling into two halves,

Compassion and Judgment.

THE CUP AT THE SIDE OF THE BED

I followed the puddle to the cloud
I followed the cloud to the well
I followed the well to the cup
At the side of the bed
Where my sister lay laboring
Her voice was my voice
But her story was not my story
I could not help her
Across the country I sat vigil
Counting petals and reciting the lessons
For the skin, calendula
For the nerves, oatstraw
Peapod for holding
Cloud for letting go

WISDOM LITERATURE

there's a dragon between my legs with one marigold eye
we didn't make the canon but we pass the wisdom down anyway
lessons of waiting for a hundred purple-black globes
to ripen lessons of gathering in the belly
raspberry leaf and red clover to feed life
knitting together white and red in darkest dark
lessons of hiddenness and scale my witches I'm just
beginning to understand we know all sorts of things
and appear in many guises like you my red-haired teacher
smoking your skinny cigarettes in the amphitheater
I wish I hadn't been so self-absorbed while I was
still your student I should have knelt before your wisdom
like a fisherman praying in a storm but that too
is wisdom literature the young missing their
lessons to make a string of mistake beads

PREGNANCY COHORT

the others have fallen

one by one

like spoken Aramaic

but we two

sing our wordless

song through blood vessels

in July

we roar across the hot street

together we are

a manatee a balloon

a cake without a birthday

a candle

MY BABY CRY

"Something cunty, something used"—Brenda Shaughnessy

I'm sorry neighbors of this borrowed

Top-floor Boston apartment

The moon absorbs his cries

And turns them to moonshine

There is a yurt in my heart

With six sides and a teak floor

The hurt of my mother

Hood on my ears he'll stop soon

Moon through the skylight

I'm sorry neighbors of this borrowed

Boston apartment

Ashamed as usual of our blood & noise

Already his cries begin to quiet

I'm hiding in the shower where he can't hear me

This is the ugliness of the mother

Something cunty, something used

I chant it to myself a witch

Cunty, used

Milk stains sweatpants

Borrowed crib crying child

SLEEP VOYAGE

Tiny white eggs in my daughter's hair

I take the long way around

We climb down to the badlands

Where a fence separates us

From men with guns

White milk spills from my baby's mouth

Onto my shirt

A lion's throat opens above us

Raw placenta meat

I bundle up my baby

Climb off the plane and kiss the red earth

THE FISH INSIDE ME

once we breathed underwater
then we crawled out of the sea
into this wet-&-dry mess
a million years learning to walk
only to turn and dive back in

for you

I've left my girlish body my
girlish mind for you I've become
ocean become whale
sifting plankton for you I glide
through time with my teeth

NEANDERTHAL DNA

Moving a box of baby clothes into the basement

I find a photograph of me at eighteen

Half my life before becoming a mother

I put it on the fridge my short greasy hair

My girl moustache

My combat boots my skirt

I love that past self now so much more

Than I loved my present self back then

And I love my current self now

I learned to love my Neanderthal DNA

By wearing myself out

Past the pretense of pluperfect

By growing a human which broke me down

Into a pile of shards pulsing with light

Now I expect to fail I expect to fuck up and

Be reprehensible I forgive myself

I know I have a moustache   it's ok

I know my heart will break again   it's ok

MY OLD AMBITION

While I still cared
About the bricks of my personality
I spent my days stacking them carefully
Around me like a chimney

Now I watch the pea shoot
Pierce the brown soil
And hurl itself towards the sun

Friend of a friend
Dying of cancer
While her four-month-old
Refuses to bottlefeed

Cornflower-blue borage
Brave radishes
Each morning I visit the sage-green

Each morning I greet
The mint jungle the shiny rosemary
Even the tiny pink saxifrage
I nurse my baby

I cannot think of my old ambition

Before my nipples darkened

QUESTIONS FROM MY UTERUS ON THE OCCASION OF MY HUSBAND'S VASECTOMY

No baby clawing at
your breast?
No baby keeping you up
all night?
No cord,
no counting
no placenta
no little toes
no hands-and-knees
no screaming
no crowning
no birth blood
no vernix?
Don't you want
to steal one more spirit
from the spirit world
and bring her down
in the form of a small body
weaving itself
of stem cells?
Don't you want
your breasts' milkswell,
netting of blue veins
across your mermaid chest?
Don't you want to plant
another grain of rice in me,
another pear, another melon?
Don't you want
to carry the mystery?

Raspberry leaf tea in the evenings
and ginger tea in the mornings?
You don't want me to be sad,
do you?
Empty sac,
all this blood
for what?

OUR OCEANGOING DAYS

I sat in the balcony waiting for you

The galley door swung on its hinges

I had to learn tolerance of uncertainty

Notes picked from air one by one

Now I bury rose quartz in the garden

I rarely call bullshit instead I walk away

Perhaps you understand

How life rears its head in the unlikeliest places

The dumpster behind the convenience store

That sells sadness

The chute that we enter in dreams

Falling through asteroid fields

Towards this oceanic planet

Where we live

Remember when we docked

On the island

Under the red velvet bedspread

I cradled you

We confessed our love

Maybe these things never happened

Maybe we never existed at all

Oh my little violin perhaps

We dreamed the ship the ocean

Our bodies the earth

ONE LAST GOODBYE

To the one who greeted me in the mirror
Who waited around the corner
Who quit this and quit that
Who started this and that
To the one who got everything she wanted
And never once realized
Extrovert introvert
Tart body pillow of the body
No-belly
Small belly
Cute belly
To the one who left
A Sumerian storm demon
Named Lilitu behind
To the one who carried my babies
Through the darkness
To the one who named them
The one who climbed the scaffolding
Of my own heart to offer sunflowers to the angry gods
The one who was alone

I bury those minutes in the garden as the baby

Grows free of his babyness

And walks away

CATHEDRAL

I type the wrong year

I hold the amethyst in my mouth

Like a sharp purple tongue

I bleed on the chair by mistake

So much blood

I make raspberry leaf tea

I make mistakes

I get a little droopy here and there

We agree on an earthquake meet-up location

We plan to stay married

I cry for the third child I don't want

And won't have

So much I could not have understood

Before turning into an asshole

So much I failed to do

When I rang the bell to the cathedral

And left my heart on the steps

Wrapped in its swaddling clothes

Once we were helpless

The house slid right off

Its foundation

The ground became water

It buckled like your hand

We are still telling the story

Even though we are

Temporarily strong

With our electric companies

And our faucets

LETTER TO THE MOON

Dear white moon in the blue July sky
you seem to be sending me a message
again, and what I hear is this will all end soon:
my young son and daughter climbing
into my bed, begging me to show them
the dinosaurs in the dinosaur book,
yellow teeth, great green bodies
rearing up above the trees, terrible
bat-wings, glowing yellow eyes
that make my children turn away
and scream in terror, joyful, maniacal,
then turn back to me, begging me
to show them the next dinosaur,
so that our morning begins in the Jurassic
age, which the book says is "much warmer
than the average temperature today
which is 57 degrees" but since it was written
five years ago that's probably inaccurate.
You know what I mean, moon, these details
asking to be savored before we melt: the grass,
bent down by small feet. The bees
nuzzling clover, playground shrieks,
blue plastic pool where we cool our ankles
and suck on lemonade popsicles
that my past self made last week.
White moon in the blue July sky, mid-day
like a warning of an era coming to a close.
Eras: Mesozoic, Anthropocene, Childhood,
Alicia. In your light, or the sun's light

that bounces through the frozen dark
of space onto you, I foresee the end,
blue like a newly washed sheet
spread smooth above us, your white
presence like the stain from two bodies
who lay on the sheet the night before
and made life between them.

Notes

BOY, GIRL, ANGEL, GOLEM

The Golem may be familiar to readers as the famous Jewish monster dating back to late-sixteenth-century Prague, a creature made of clay by Rabbi Judah Lowe, and sometimes considered the inspiration for Mary Wollstonecraft Shelley's *Frankenstein*. This famously powerful-yet-unintelligent monster is dear to my heart; for eight years I played in a klezmer-punk band named Golem. However, this particular poem draws instead on the earlier origins of the word:

From *Wikipedia*: "The word *golem* occurs once in the Bible in Psalm 139:16, which uses the word גלמי (*galmi; my golem*), that means 'my light form,' 'raw' material, connoting the unfinished human being before God's eyes . . . In the Talmud (Tractate Sanhedrin 38b), Adam was initially created as a golem (גולם) when his dust was 'kneaded into a shapeless husk.'"

MAGIC MOVES FROM SIDE TO SIDE

Inspired in part by the story of Tamar and Judah (Genesis 38), and of course, potty training.

More on Tamar, adapted from the *Girls in Trouble Curriculum*, also written by Alicia Jo Rabins: "Tamar marries two Israelite brothers, one after another, each of whom dies by the hand of God. After these episodes, her father-in-law Judah is afraid to lose a third son and withholds him from Tamar, although by ancient law she should have been able to marry him, since she does not have a child by either of the first two brothers. This series of events leaves Tamar seemingly powerless: a woman alone in a patriarchal society with no husband or children. Tamar responds by hiding her face beneath a veil and waiting at the crossroads where she knows Judah will be passing to shear his sheep. When he passes by, she seduces him, and becomes pregnant with twins, from whom the line of the Messiah will eventually descend. I am captivated by the mysteries and transformations of this encounter."

LAMENT FOR THE PRE-PREGNANCY CITY

Thanks to Lower Manhattan Cultural Council for the Workspace grant, which offers artists access to unused office space near Wall Street; I wrote in one of those semi-abandoned offices in 2009–2010.

THE VAGINA HEALER

This poem is inspired by the work of Tami Kent, MSPT, a writer, healer and physical therapist specializing in the pelvic floor.

REMEMBER HOW WE PLANNED...

This poem is for Peter Avniel Salzman z"l, 1975–2013.

MY NEW FACE

Jazz-trained drummers often have a distinctive way of playing, similar to classically trained musicians, as opposed to rock-trained or self-taught drummers.

ANCESTOR ALPHABET

Aleph, Lamed, Tzadi and *Hay* are four of the twenty-two Hebrew letters. "Final" tzadi is the term for when this letter appears at the end of a word and is written differently (as some Hebrew letters are).

Asherah is an ancient near eastern goddess, worshipped by the cultures out of which the Ancient Israelite culture arose. The Hebrew Bible specifically forbids the worship of Asherah by name, repeatedly, which perhaps implies there was still a significant desire to continue worshipping her.

ISIS LACTANS

The title refers to the name for an ancient figurine of the goddess Isis, depicted breastfeeding.

From Johns Hopkins's Archaeological Museum website: "The goddess Isis was perhaps the most important goddess in the Egyptian pantheon. She was primarily a maternal goddess of magic. Amulets of Isis were extremely common, and by the Late Period (ca. 664–332 BCE), they could be found on almost every mummy. One of Isis's most popular amuletic forms was as a lactating woman, nursing her son, Horus-the-Child, the god of divine kingship."

THE MONASTERY OF MOTHERHOOD
"El Shaddai" is one of the many names for God in the Torah. There are various interpretations of the name; this poem follows the translation of "El Shaddai" as "God of the Breast."

From *Wikipedia*: "An alternative view . . . is that the name is connected to *shadayim* which means "pair of breasts" in Hebrew (from *shad*, breast, and *ai-im*, an ending signifying a dual noun). It may thus be connected to the notion of God's fertility and blessings to humanity. In several instances it is connected with fruitfulness: 'May God Almighty [El Shaddai] bless you and make you fruitful and increase your numbers . . .' (Gen. 28:3). 'I am God Almighty [El Shaddai]: be fruitful and increase in number' (Gen. 35:11). 'By the Almighty [Shaddai] who will bless you with blessings of heaven above, blessings of the deep that lies beneath, blessings of the breasts and of the womb' . . . (Gen. 49:25). Harriet Lutzky has presented evidence that Shaddai was an attribute of a Semitic goddess, linking the epithet with Hebrew *šad* 'breast' as 'the one of the Breast,' as Asherah at Ugarit is 'the one of the Womb.'"

CRADLE CAP
The title refers to a very common, nondangerous condition among newborns in which their scalp skin becomes very dry and the top layer begins to peel off.

MEMOIR
The kabbalists divide the world into two main impulses: Compassion (*Chesed*) and Judgment (*Din*). We are challenged to balance the two.

MY BABY CRY
The Brenda Shaughnessy quotation is from her poem "Liquid Flesh," from *Our Andromeda* (Copper Canyon Press, 2012).

NEANDERTHAL DNA

LA Times, October 5, 2017: "Altogether, scientists now estimate that somewhere between 1.8% and 2.6% of the DNA in most people alive today was inherited from Neanderthals, according to a report published Thursday in the journal *Science*."

ONE LAST GOODBYE

The Sumerian storm demoness *Lilitu* is thought to be the origin for the apocryphal Jewish legend of Lilith, a favorite of mine.

More on Lilith, adapted from the *Girls in Trouble Curriculum*: "Lilith is considered by mystics to be the proto-Eve created in the first creation story in Genesis, in which God creates a single human and then splits them in two. She considers herself equal to Adam and, for this presumption, is banished from Eden, after which God creates Eve from Adam's rib in the second creation story. Lilith has been an outsized presence in the minds and hearts of esoteric kabbalists and ordinary women, and not always in a good way. Lilith was a terrifying figure for medieval Jews; to keep her away, they chanted poems containing her name during sex and childbirth, and wore amulets with her name to guard themselves. Over the course of three thousand years, Lilith has played wildly different roles in both Jewish and non-Jewish imaginations. A terrifying demoness and dangerous temptress in the ancient and medieval world; a fetishized object in nineteenth-century paintings; a feisty symbol of women's liberation in the 1970s. To follow this journey is to experience a prism of relationships to female power."

CATHEDRAL

This poem is inspired by the Cascadia Earthquake, aka the Big One, which geologists say is overdue in the Pacific Northwest.

From the *New Yorker*, July 20, 2015: "An earthquake will destroy a sizable portion of the coastal Northwest. The question is when."

Acknowledgments

Thanks to the following publications in which these poems first appeared (sometimes under different titles):

Academy of American Poets' *Poem-A-Day*: Geode

American Poetry Review: I Dream of My Baby Sleeping While He Sleeps, My New Face, Passenger, Pig in a Blanket, Questions from My Uterus on the Occasion of My Husband's Vasectomy, Remember How We Planned to Get Married and Have Children?

The Collagist: Home Birth Videos

Ilanot Review: Goodbye to the One I Was, The Cup at the Side of the Bed

Jai-Alai: Materia Medica

Mantis: Babies in the Apocalypse, Beautiful Virus

No Tokens: Lament for the Pre-pregnancy City, The Monastery of Motherhood

Obey Much, Resist Little: Inaugural Poems to the Resistance (anthology from Spuyten Duyvil Press): The Black Box, Mothersickness, Song of Praise

Tin House: Cathedral, The Vagina Healer, We Learn to Be Human

Willow Springs Review: The Fish Inside Me

Zócalo Public Square: When I Lived in New York

Heartfelt Thanks

My beloved Sylvia and Elijah, for being your glorious selves, being my teachers, and making me a mother. My mother, who gave birth to me at home in Portland, Oregon, on Valentine's Day. My sisters, father, grandparents, great-grandparents, and all the ancestors.

Kate Angus, editor of my dreams (and so much more) and Joe Pan, publisher extraordinaire.

The Peleh Fellowship, for invaluable support and encouragement; the Residency on Prince Street, for the gift of writing time and child care; and Joshua Venture Group and the Covenant Foundation for support and mentorship. These extraordinary gifts allowed me to keep making art with small children; I am grateful.

The Grind and its fearless leader Ross White, without which this book would literally not exist; Jennifer Sweeney and Hoa Nguyen (for the edits); Portland's Poetry Press Week, for bringing these poems to life onstage.

My midwife, Dr. Mary, and the midwives and neonatal nurses at Legacy Emanuel.

Dear friends who helped with this book: Megan Wechsler, Malinda Allen, Annette Ezekiel Kogan, Filip Marinovich, Abigail Susik Browning, Ruth Wikler, Penelope Rose Miller, Julianna Bright, Ana Helena de Castro, Jane Gottesman and the Biddle-Gottesman clan, the poet-moms listserv, and my writing group brothers and sisters: Chrys Tobey, Jesse Lichtenstein, Elizabeth T. Gray Jr, Abby Wender, Maeve Kinkead, JJ Penna, Matt Minicucci, Vandoren Wheeler, David Naimon.

My teachers, too many to name here.

To all the mamas—past present and future—and the wise women, midwives, healers, witches.

And again, to Aaron—you are the love of my life.

About the Author

Alicia Jo Rabins is a poet, musician, composer, and Torah scholar. She teaches ancient Jewish texts to children and adults and performs internationally as a violinist and singer. Alicia's first book, *Divinity School*, was selected by C. D. Wright for the APR/ Honickman First Book Prize. She lives in Portland, Oregon with her partner and two children.

CPSIA information can be obtained
at www.ICGtesting.com
Printed in the USA
FSHW02n0242140718
50273FS